LIMITLESS

Sharing The Wor(l)d Through Love's Eyes

LIMITLESS

Sharing The Wor(l)d Through Love's Eyes

20 empowering poems
for free use in
retreats, classrooms, webinars, seminars, book clubs,
online courses and other creative projects.

Sadhbh Adamea

Love-Eyes Spiritual Development

LIMITLESS. Sharing The Wor(l)d Through Love's Eyes

Formatting template by Derek Murphy of Creativindie Design.
Cover and interior design by the author. Cover picture taken by the author.

For information contact :

http://www.love-eyes.com

Tradepaper ISBN: 978-1-0687792-0-6

10 9 8 7 6 5 4 3 2 1

1st edition, September 2024

For Love

This book contains workbook pages.
You can download these pages separately
as a PDF to print them for yourself
or for use with your groups.

Just scan this code and enter the password:
limitless

FOREWORD

Sadhbh's poetry is a sacred ritual, a meditation in words. Her verses are an invitation to slow down and inhabit the present with a sense of wonder. With each line, she unveils a new facet of our shared humanity, offering solace and inspiration.

Her work is a testament to the power of the human spirit to find beauty in the ordinary. Sadhbh invites us to cultivate a deeper connection to nature and ourselves. Her poetry is a gentle reminder that even in the midst of life's challenges, there is magic to be found.

It's been an honor to get to know her through her poetry. I feel like I've been given a peak into a wonderful world, one that sees the fruit that all experience can bear.

Sadhbh's unwavering pursuit of authenticity shines through in every word. Her poetry is a gentle invitation to explore the depths of your own soul. To read her words is to embark on a poetic journey, one that will awaken you to the songs your own heart carries.

Emily O' Neal

WHO OWNS THE WOR(L)D?

"In the beginning was the Word, and the Word was with God, and the Word was God." John 1.1

I ALWAYS LOVED WORDS. I not only loved to talk, I also loved to write. I loved wordplay and playing with words and although I didn't really enjoy the stale linguistics class that was part of my English studies, I love looking at the deeper meaning and etymology of a word.

We learn to speak, and depending on how we grow up, our inner dictionary evolves. It keeps on growing as we read. Conversations transform our vocabulary. Television and interactions on social media constantly add new expressions and words to our human lexicon. Every subsequent generation creates new words - like everything, the world of words is in constant flow.

We use and understand language on a very personal level. Everyone knows that feeling of having been in a conversation and not feeling understood, although hours have passed by while talking. Sometimes we feel that we use the right words, yet it seems the other person is hearing it all differently. We are desperate to be understood. However, words carry different meanings. Dependent on how we were brought up, one word can mean something entirely different to us than to our friend, spouse or colleague.

True understanding happens beyond words, in the space between words, and in the energy created by those words. This is where poetry can travel worlds and be understood through frequency. Have you ever read a poem in another language and still felt the underlying energy of this poem? When we create art from a flow state, we tap into the very source that we are made of: LOVE.
(Every time I am referring to this universal, non-cloaked understanding of the word, it will be capitalized.)

THIS LOVE CAN WRAP THE SOULS OF THE AUTHOR, READER AND LISTENER IN AWE AND WONDER. WE CREATE AN ENERGY FIELD THROUGH ART.

As a writer, I express myself through words. I am mainly inspired by that inner source that flows through me and makes my fingers fly across the keyboard or paper. What would my words look like if I hadn't accumulated a lifetime of other people's words, witnessed other people's actions, or seen other people's ideas? What would my words sound like, if I hadn't seen other people's creations? What would my words mirror, if I hadn't observed nature, the animal world and mankind? Everything I am right now leads to how I write. If I had to give credit to everyone that inspired me to write this very book, the book would probably be as big as the bible, as every tiny interaction in my life has influenced me to become the person that I am right now. Every word that I heard from another was processed inside my brain and labeled with a certain meaning, due to the way I have lived till now. We live within a limitless tapestry of words that weaves us into a big interconnected story. How do we know where the thread begins? How do we know who said what first?

Before the invention of the internet, we could look at books and the years they were written in, and we could speculate who came up with a certain quote first. How many books were destroyed though? How many books have never been written? How many words have been put down in writing by someone else other than the inventor of the idea?

We can try to own a word or a quote. We can try to make ourselves special. We can put laws on it and spend our energy fighting others, just to be able to say "I was there first.". If, like the quote earlier stated, "God is the word", we can't possess it. God is Love. We can't possess Love. Isn't the purpose of a book, especially spiritual books, to inspire people, to wake them up to Love? Don't we want Love spread uncontrollably? Where does this need to protect "our" words come from?

I was called to write this book in this form after a painful encounter with the human copyright laws. Floating in an unconditional Love and awe for other creators, my understanding of the laws of the universe clashed with man-made laws. I felt confused and ashamed, not having faced "reality" before. This moment catapulted me into the deepest shadows of my ego. Although I had nothing but good intentions, the shame around this incident was so crushing that I almost stopped writing. I wished to disappear into other realms immediately. Every challenge comes with a gift, and thus, this incident caused me to rethink how I want to show up as an author. From my deep dive into spiritual practices, I already knew how our ego strives to possess, to hold on and to be special. For me, sharing someone's words was an act of Love. Reciting my favourite poem or quoting a beautiful passage of someone's teachings could in my mind just benefit the author, as I always referred to them. In times of Instagram and TikTok, quotes and memes travel through space, carrying the intention to uplift, inspire and celebrate words. In this web of sharing, how do we even pinpoint the source? As I dove deeper into our world's copyright laws, I froze. Technically, due to the fact that every artist's work is automatically copyrighted, nobody is allowed to take any of the words I am writing here or on Instagram and share them without my permission. In our money-making focused world, everyone wants a piece of the cake and, therefore, there are laws that protect our "rights". I don't understand how this is benefitting anyone.

If our ancestors hadn't shared stories around the fire and someone else hadn't shared them with their kids, how would they have kept the words alive? How do we celebrate a poet or an author without cherishing their words by sharing? How can we let poetry stir our blood if nobody reads the words out loud? If someone wrote a piece of poetry that touched my heart, isn't it a good thing if I share it with others? Isn't this an act of Love? Isn't it an honour if someone quotes our wise words and gives a shout-out to the author? Of course, to merely copy someone's work and put one's own name underneath would be unethical. Yet, if someone decides to do it, I can not control that. I can only control my reaction. In a rapidly evolving online world, where machines can now easily put together a sonnet, I think it is foolish to spend my energy chasing the ones that decide to create from fear. In my mind, Karma takes care of such things anyway. After soothing my nervous system through my daily mindfulness practices, I was able to alchemize the fear, shame and confusion into Love. A desire arose. A desire to make my words available for the world to use. A desire to write this book.

Shame. When I look at this word, I naturally cringe. I think of the million ways in which we get shamed and shame ourselves for who we are. We get shamed and shame ourselves for not having enough, for not doing enough, for not being enough and for not knowing enough. We get shamed and shame ourselves for being too much, for making mistakes, for not thinking like someone else. The list is endless. Our negatively biased brain easily focusses on limitations, lack and separation. The daily news, advertisements and social media posts almost make it hard for us to escape the "reality" of the "terrible state of the world". However, what we focus on, we get more of. I have made "seeing the world through the eyes of Love" my daily practice. It even became my way of living and how I see the world. As many people are used to focusing on the things that are wrong with this world, my worldview is often labeled as naive. The word "naive" in its original connotation means as much as "natural". A perfect example of how we put meaning on words, although their innate meaning draws quite a different picture. So, I believe, seeing the world through Love's eyes is natural. This is my truth.

Who gets to decide what's right or wrong? I believe that we have an innate compass of what is right or wrong. You may not agree with this, as clearly it seems like there are people who exploit the generous, take from the poor and do all kinds of "wrong" things that make our hearts scream in agony. The worst part is they don't even seem to care. Yet, we can never look inside a person and know for sure how they feel. I believe that it is not necessary for us to judge someone's behaviour, and that doing so does not serve us either. When we judge a person, our energy level lowers, we cut ourselves off from the source that we are and we get stuck in a negative thinking cycle. Thus, I believe that everyone is responsible for their own emotions, their own actions and how we show up in the world is what the world mirrors back to us.

However, copyright laws are part of this human experience. I, as the author of this book though, have the right to decide not to give a sh* if someone doesn't credit me. Of course, I also believe that it would be closer to Love to say where the words are cited from.

I want you to do what you feel compelled to do with this book and the words in it, without feeling shame or worrying if you quoted correctly. I want you to be able to enjoy this Love infused book to the fullest. Therefore, you are allowed to share these words without limits. Shout them out loud or recite them in silence, read them, take them in, make quotes of them or give them away. The only thing I would ask you is to always make sure you are spreading these words as an act of Love. How do you know? If you feel good about it, if every part of your body and soul screams: Yes! That's the right thing to do! Then you are most certainly acting out of Love.

Our body shows us the way. Deep inside yourself you know what is right or wrong for you. I don't know if you have the means to buy this book. I don't know your mission. I don't know your values, your lifestyle, or your intentions. This book is for the world to read. These words are for the world to feel. To be experienced. You can use them for yourself, for groups, classrooms, retreats, the list is limitless.

Don't get me wrong, I am not condoning literary theft, however, feel free to quote anything you like. If my poems inspire you to get creative, if you, for example, make an Instagram reel, reading my poetry, then you are putting your own energy and work into it. Of course, if you gave me credit for the energy I put into these words, you would double the Love you are spreading. Pouring your own perception and the wisdom that you've gained throughout your life into your art, is not imitating, but creating. So go ahead and get creative!

If you want to support my work, you are always welcome to make a donation! In fact, I'd appreciate that very much. There are many ways to give back to something that we have received. There is Love and appreciation, spreading the word, sending gifts, crafting something, writing a note or a letter, offering your own services to the one who gave you something, listening, being a friend, exchanging a physical item for what you've received ..., - the possibilities are limitless.

Money is energy and so is Love. Therefore, I appreciate any kind of energy exchange for the energy that flew through me onto these pages. You reading this book is an energy exchange in itself, even if it has been gifted to you, as without you as a reader, I could not be of service. I have learned that energy does not necessarily flow back to the place where it comes from. If you use the words from this book to spread some Love, I know that this Love will come back to me tenfold in other ways. So please go on and spread these words, let us leave a trail of Love wherever we go.

CONTENTS

My currency is Love

and I'm spending it all

on you!

INTRODUCTION

THE POETRY I WRITE is the language of my essence, the language of Love. I alone can't take credit for the poetry that I capture, as I am just the vessel through which the words flow. I am the pen-holder, the fingers that type, the body that is so beautifully crafted that I can put those ideas and words on paper. I could have made this book available for free download as a simple PDF file. Why didn't I do it?

In times of e-readers and audiobooks, there is a reason why a solid book in our hands is still preferred by so many of us. Books are like a good friend that is always at our side. I especially like books that tickle the mind and nourish the soul. When you are holding this book in your hand, you are not only touching a book. You are touching pages made of wood, part of nature. Everything is vibration; thus, this book is the physical realization of an idea that is carrying vibration. The words printed on paper carry their own vibration. The poetry in this book transports vibration when it is recited. The paper itself reverberates this very frequency. Empowering stories, magical tales, helpful conversations, interesting rituals and soulful words - when books are written in a poetic way, with a reverence towards every single word, when I, as a reader, can feel the sacredness of every tiny letter, the reading experience is beyond pleasure. To cherish nature for providing this book's paper, a part of its profit will be donated to a tree planting organization.

***

It is elevating to read a good book. Time stands still. Reading can be a meditation in itself. Books carry a vibration. They are much like taking the hand of a parent, and being guided home. I am constantly in awe of how books find me in so many wonderful ways. At times, the cover shines at me in a bookstore, catching my eye, calling me to take it home. It doesn't even have to be pretty; it can just be the way the words are arranged or the way the colours are displayed. Other times, books find me through people, telling me about a good read. Every day I go to my bookshelf, listening to the little voice that guides me to the book that is answering the feeling that I carried in my heart, to the stillness that is needed in my mind, and to the questions that my soul wants to live. Books are friends, lovers, parents, companions and sometimes maps to a realm of what has not yet been explored.

There is magic inside of a book. I believe that the magic of the author's soul is dancing in between the syllables, the spaces and the sounds of the words. Do you hear the traces of starry glitter when you hold a book to your ear? Do you catch yourself caressing your favourite book?

This is because the relationship with a book can be very intimate. The secrets that the words hold, may just be the key to your heart. That key may unlock a journey that you've never even dared to dream. That key may allow your soul to take in the wisdom of the universe, which had spoken through the author's pen. The wisdom of someone who felt compelled to tell their story, to speak their truth, to create wizardry, and wise art, contained between pages that smell of change and transformation. The sound of a marker engraving the words into your being. The taste of alchemy on your tongue. The privilege of taking the time to sit in silence with a book in hand in an always busy world. Reminding you that the present moment is the only way home.

HOW TO READ THIS BOOK

There are so many ways to read a book. You can start from the beginning and read it till the end. You can start in the middle and then come back to the beginning later. You can start at the end and read backwards. I love to flip books open, because the universe always guides me to the pages that are meant for me at this very moment. If you are using this book in retreats, classrooms or other groups, the page you are flipping open might be exactly the one that someone needs to hear. You can also do this with just one sentence.

You can use this book to grow yourself, as I included pages with questions to ponder after every poem. Those questions are an invitation to dive deeper into the main topic of the poem. Feel free to add your own questions, to alter the existing ones or leave some of them out. Maybe the answers come to you in a poem. It is most beneficial to journal about these questions. However, if you want to discuss them in a group setting, that can be very insightful, too. I would recommend not rushing through the questions, but pondering each of them individually, maybe even for several days. If you want to explore the questions in a group setting, you can download a journal with the questions only via the QR code that is to be found in the beginning of the book.

You can highlight, take notes or read every line and let it sink in for several minutes. You can use the poem titles to write your own version. You can extract your favourite quote from the poem. You can recite the poem at an open mic night, practicing speaking in public until you are ready to spread your own words. You can take the poem and make art from it. You can paint or draw the poem. You can take a picture of something inspired by the poem. You can dance the poem or make a song out of it. You can learn it by heart and carry its energy with you, wherever you go. You can use it as a prayer. You can take the words, shake them all up and create a new poem. You can make reels or TikTok videos out of them. You can read them to elderly, children, teens, and people in need. You can use them to shamelessly remind everyone that they are the Love they are searching for. The possibilities are limitless.

If you use these words mindfully, nothing can go wrong. Let's take "money rules the world" and give it its truthful meaning: Love rules the world! This is our chance to make an impact! Let's never waste our creativity to fear.

***

This book is infused with powerful poetry. Poetry, that I mainly write to process my own feelings. It often feels like some universal voice speaks to me through the words of poetry. I find comfort and empowerment in my own poetry, and I believe that these are the words of the universe, telling me that she has my back. I want to share these encouraging poems with you. May they embrace you with comfort, Love and the feeling of empowerment.

Poetry helps us to dive deep into our inner worlds. We step across a threshold through the arch of each letter of the alphabet, finding ourselves in another dimension. Words carry vibration and poetry creates a unique magical power through the interplay of rhythm, rhyme, pace, metaphor and sound. We are used to escaping our own feelings. Society trains us to numb our pain instead of feeling it. In the comfort and embrace of a poem, we can safely explore our emotions and let them run through our bodies. We can then let them go and find ourselves refreshed and cleansed.

Poetry is a spiritual practice.

PART I:

I Have Enough

From an early age on, we are trained to focus on lack.

"This is yours, and this is mine," is one of the earliest things we learn while sharing the sandbox with other children. Separation and an overly heightened awareness of our ego is the result. We start embarking on the journey to search on the outside for what can only be found on the inside.

Lackful thinking increases through advertisements and a societal fear of not having enough money, resources, or time. We go through life, constantly trying to control what is happening around us, and cling to what we have already gained or possess in fear of losing it, when nothing in life is truly permanent.

Reminding ourselves that we always have enough, and focusing on what we have instead of what we don't have can make a huge impact. Love is always abundant. Love doesn't get less when we give it away. We might as well relax into her arms and tell ourselves gently:

I HAVE ENOUGH!

MY CURRENCY IS LOVE

My currency is Love.

I pay
in kind words
and glowing smiles

my light
the energy
that flows
from the inside
towards the sky
so that you
if passing by
are baptized
in the golden shower
of appreciation
and gratitude
for being
you

My currency
is Love
and I'm spending
it all on you

Love-Eyes Exercise

What is your relationship with money?

Love-Eyes Exercise

Where have you witnessed the loving energy of money?

Love-Eyes Exercise

Which relationship do you want to have with money?

Love-Eyes Exercise

What would you do with your life,
if your well-being and financial safety
were taken care of?

EXPERIENCE

We sleep, we crawl, we walk
We learn how to smile, how to talk
And when we think, we got it all
we suddenly stumble and fall

When we are children, we just try again
We don't judge ourselves for falling down
We scream and we cry, but then we get up
We simply adjust the invisible crown

We learn to fear the painful times
Somehow, somewhere, along the way
We pick up beliefs and fill our minds
Until we hear this voice discerningly say

Why did you fall? Couldn't you do better?
We start to feel shameful and almost give up
As the feelings grow stronger, fueling the chatter
We turn towards anything for our brain to stop

No one is judging our setbacks and failures
except for our own critical voice
Yet, all it takes is self-compassion
We have the power; we can make the choice

Let's simply observe our mistakes and missteps
Let's find out what life is teaching us to do
Self-Love and patience are the key to success
That's how we make our dreams come true

Love-Eyes Exercise

What is your relationship with judgement?

Love-Eyes Exercise

Do you fear being judged?

Love-Eyes Exercise

Do you judge often?

Love-Eyes Exercise

Which relationship do you want to have with judgement?

Love-Eyes Exercise

What would your life look like
if you didn't fear being judged?

Love-Eyes Exercise

How would your relationships change
if you didn't judge?

Love-Eyes Exercise

Can you witness your judgement without judgement?

RIPPED OPEN

And your doubts can become a gift
showing up at your doorstep
unannounced
huge
beautifully wrapped

You stare at the hard cardboard
in disbelief of its sudden appearance.

It's hard to find the spot
this little spot
where your fingers
find the beginning

Impatiently
you fiddle with the tape
examining the shape.

It looks eerily familiar

For a short moment
you stop

–

suddenly
afraid
of what could hide inside

It smells
of childhood dreams
and shattered pride
and still
you decide
to stay curious

slowly unpacking
layer by layer
in your heart
a silent prayer
for bravery

Time flies by
the rhythmical sound
of ripping cardboard
playing the song
of patience
as one by one
you set free
the glistening treasures:

confidence
courage
insight
understanding
compassion
kindness
love

As the river
of relief
emerges from your eyes
you look at the ripped parts
of the package,
the lies
that covered the treasure
of your heart

And you rise

Never again
to fall apart

Love-Eyes Exercise

How comfortable are you with exploring your negative feelings?

Love-Eyes Exercise

How comfortable are you with enjoying your positive feelings?

Love-Eyes Exercise

Which feeling can you unwrap curiously today?

Love-Eyes Exercise

Which feelings do you have boxed
and stored away?
Which can you take out to explore?

Love-Eyes Exercise

Where does a stored feeling live in your body?

SEASONS OF THE SOUL

You can't bring back the spring
that let your heart blossom
just because it seems too hard
to deal with the darkness of winter

You can't bring back the buds
of new beginnings
when the process is on its way
of unfolding

A tree cannot grow new leaves
if it doesn't let go of the old ones

So darling, please breathe deeply
and surrender to the pain
of letting go.

The next spring is just around the corner
and the roses will bloom even more fully
The beauty of spring always shows up
No matter how cold and hard the winter has been

Every tiny change needs to be seen.
Every leaf that falls to the ground
becomes part of the nourishing soil
and blends into the mud
that covers the root with softness and care

Every season has its purpose
and so does every part of your soul
Only by accepting the cycle of the seasons
You can find your inner being whole

Love-Eyes Exercise

What is your relationship with change?

Love-Eyes Exercise

How practiced are you in letting go of people, circumstances, things you can't change?

Love-Eyes Exercise

Which relationship do you want to have with change?

Love-Eyes Exercise

How can you strengthen your faith in the unfolding of life for your highest good?

Love-Eyes Exercise

How can you practice accepting what is?

SIGNS

Child
of the earth
let your tears flow
let them clear your vision
as you let them go
let yourself be carried
by the storm's
strong embrace
the squeaking trees
leading with grace
as they twist and turn
and dance

Every step
a choice
every move
a chance
let yourself be carried away
into the air of possibilities
to rise above the limits of your mind
for weightlessness
bears freedom

Trust
the universe
is always kind
your soul has wings
that help you land on solid ground
as you stand breathless
deeply in awe
feel energy inside, around

When calm hits water
you will receive
how to align
as you believe
you'll get your sign
a bird, a word
a deer, a sound
follow their lead
don't hesitate
just go
trust that they know
which paths you need
to fully bloom
to always grow

Love-Eyes Exercise

How can you expand tiny moments of bliss that you feel in our life?

Love-Eyes Exercise

What are your beliefs about the world? Do you believe the world is safe and kind or dark and cruel?

Love-Eyes Exercise

How do your current beliefs serve you?
What are they keeping you from?

Love-Eyes Exercise

How can you shift your belief
or strengthen it?

Love-Eyes Exercise

How can you trust more in your own energy?

PART II:

I Do Enough

Our modern world is always in motion.

At the beginning of the year, we set intentions, strive for goals, wanting to get better, improving ourselves, working day and night and finally losing ourselves in the rat race of life. We seldom give ourselves permission to stop and breathe.

When we are on holidays, we fall into a kind of rigor mortis, overeating and lying at the beach until the sun leaves her marks on our backs, imprinting us with the falsely tanned statement of: I took care of myself. We work to live, we live to work, yet we can achieve so much more by simply being. The present moment holds magical powers.

If we practice bringing our awareness to the here and now, our energy naturally rises. We cease to feel the need to control, as in the present moment we are safe and well. Mindfulness practices not only calm us down, they also improve our health and overall well-being. Wouldn't it feel better to be totally calm in the middle of the storm and let go instead of trying to react to an uncontrollable situation? Let us relax for a moment and tell ourselves kindly:

I DO ENOUGH!

MOUNTAINEER

When the clouds
above your head
weigh heavy
and their darkness
seems to swallow
your mind,
lower your gaze
towards your feet

It was here
where you started
It was them
who first brought you forward
just to carry you since then

And are we not too often
focused on the top?
On getting there quickly
to enjoy the view
when on our way
towards the top
there's so much to see

It all starts with you

For without you
the top will never be climbed
It is not the fear
of never getting there
that takes you to the top

It is the anticipation,
the Love you feel
for the view
although you haven't been there
This is the energy
that makes your feet
keep going
although the incline
is steep

The top will never be climbed
without a steady ground
without a nourished body
and the relentless
navigation through obstacles

So, focus
on the foundation
and then
step back
to watch the beauty
of the unknown
with fascination

Be curious,
be patient,
for all the clouds
will eventually
give way
to the sun

Sometimes
by standing still
you get a lot more done

Love-Eyes Exercise

Where do you pressure yourself to take action?

Love-Eyes Exercise

How can you give yourself permission to take a break more often?

Love-Eyes Exercise

What is your relationship with the unknown?

Love-Eyes Exercise

How can you have more mindful moments throughout your day?

COME SIT WITH ME I

Come

Come and sit with me
in stillness
let your feelings come and go,
let our connection flow,
just you and me
and the stunning sea

Come sit with me
in peace
let your feelings go and come
let us realize we are one
everyone
and you
and me
nature, animals and the sea

Come sit with me

Love-Eyes Exercise

How can you ground yourself more often?

Love-Eyes Exercise

When was the last time you were in nature?

Love-Eyes Exercise

When was the last time you visited the ocean?

Love-Eyes Exercise

How does the ocean's ebb and flow mirror the movement in your own life?

COME SIT WITH ME II

Come

Come and sit with me
in stillness
-
while the morning
greets the new day
Let your heart run free
across fields of gold
enjoy yourself
like the playing deer
Listen to your soul
as they disappear
into the shelter
of the trees
Find the humming of the bees
singing to your heart
about all the possibilities
this new day brings forth
Come and sit with me
watch the fog
covering the soft waves
dancing
in between the creases
as the night
slowly deceases
and makes room
for the day ahead
Come sit with me
and meditate
in nature's bed

Love-Eyes Exercise

When was the last time you
watched the sunrise?

Love-Eyes Exercise

How can you pay more attention to the wild animals and their signs?

Love-Eyes Exercise

Can you imagine hugging a tree?
Can you try it?

Love-Eyes Exercise

How can you appreciate the little insects that are accompanying you in nature?

Love-Eyes Exercise

What can fog teach us?

COME SIT WITH ME III

Come

Come and sit with me
at the stunning lake
let us keep wake
for all the broken dreams
and tearful sorrows

Come sit with me
let us breathe
together
let us feel the pain
of loneliness like rain
dripping down on our souls
unyielding, unsettling

Come sit with me
and feel the presence
of Love
Glistening
underneath the calm
surface of the water
Feel the roots of
connection beneath
the earth

Come sit with me

Love-Eyes Exercise

When was the last time you were at a lake?

Love-Eyes Exercise

How does calm water mirror parts of your life?

Love-Eyes Exercise

How long can you stare at a lake?

Love-Eyes Exercise

How does a lake throughout the seasons change?
How can that depict parts of your life?

INVITATION

Sit down
relax
and then become still

so still
that beyond
your heartbeat
you can hear
the mice breathing
in their morning meditation

so still
that you can hear
the bugs chewing
their breakfast

so still
that you can hear the water
softening the skin of driftwood

so still
that you can hear the trees
bowing their violins of wisdom

so still
that you can hear
the trees drinking
their morning elixir

Relax your gaze
let your eyes rest
and widen
your perspective

so wide
that you can see
the fish breathing

so wide
that you can see
a bee
resting peacefully
on the swaying grass
far away - in the distance

so wide
that you can spot
the animals
that are perfectly
blending with the scenery

so wide
that you can see up to the top
of the highest tree

so wide
that you can see
the wind caressing
the surface of the water
translating vibration
into the rhythm
of the earth

Free
your nose
breathe in deeply

so deep
that you can smell
the composition
of nature's
very own perfume

so deep
that you can scent
the luscious greens
combined with sweet
blossoms of spring
the underlying trace
of musty sand
perfecting the experience

so deep
that you can smell
the ointment
of the precious well
giving life
to animals and plants
casting a powerful
spell

Open your mouth
and let your tongue
taste
the delicious flavour
of the world's biggest buffet

savour the honey
of every sweet bud
the bitter plants
the spicy poisons
and the healing herbs

taste
life's variety
showing off
endless possibilities
as the sun
mulls the exuberance
of nourishing plants
into liquid gold

Sharpen your sense

feel the space
surrounding your soul
expanding
melting
with the spirit
of Mother Earth

feel the soul
of nature
lying her blanket
around your heart
from there you start
into a new day
from there
you will find
your wild and peaceful way

Love-Eyes Exercise

How can you use your senses more to experience mindful moments?

Love-Eyes Exercise

Which is your favourite sense?

Love-Eyes Exercise

Which of your senses gets quickly overwhelmed?

Love-Eyes Exercise

How can you sense more deeply?

Love-Eyes Exercise

How comfortable are you with silence?

PART III:

I Am Enough

Life is a journey from imitation to creation.

After we pick up all kinds of fears, beliefs, conditions and dreams of others, we suddenly wake up and realize that we don't know who we really are. In our desperate search for belonging, we look outside of ourselves for validation. This leads to a huge fear of judgement and rejection.

We don't dare to live our true authentic self as we fear to be too much, too loud, too quiet, too different, too special, not enough. We are disconnected from our inner wisdom and turn to others for advice and comfort. When we strip down all the layers, explore who we really are and dare to sing our own songs, our soul unfolds and shines brightly.

Self-compassion helps us to forgive grievances and let the past no longer write our future stories.
We then recognize our own face in the mirror of another person, and we discover the truth:

I AM ENOUGH!

CARVINGS

I've carved
the journey
of my soul
in wood
with a steady hand
taking care
of all the details

Every curve
and every ornament
carefully placed
in exactly the right
moment

My hands run over the wood
feeling all the highs and lows
the ups and downs
tracing the lines with my finger

Slowly I am stepping back
content with the result
my eyes touching the warm
colours
indulging in the scent
a work in progress
embracing the change
to become
a unique
piece of art
made by Love
    - created by my heart

Love-Eyes Exercise

What is your relationship to yourself?

Love-Eyes Exercise

How do you witness talking to yourself?

Love-Eyes Exercise

Which relationship do you want to have with yourself?

Love-Eyes Exercise

How would your life change
if you were as compassionate with yourself
as with others?

YOUR SOUL'S GARDEN

Dig deep
into the soil
Get your hands dirty
Pull out the roots
that are no longer needed

Water your plants
the old and the new
As long as you flow
your garden will grow

Prune your branches
just to let them sprout
so that they can reach out
to the sky

Enjoy the little helpers
listen to the buzz and the birds
cherish all the work they're doing
as they run and fly

Finally sit still
enjoy the scents, the colours the view
relax into this blessed moment
of being in your soul's garden
of being authentically you

Love-Eyes Exercise

What is your relationship with growth?

Love-Eyes Exercise

How are you witnessing your own growth?

Love-Eyes Exercise

Which relationship do you want to have with growth?

Love-Eyes Exercise

How would your life change,
if you gave yourself more time to savour
and cherish your growth?

LIFE IS YOUR SONG

Don't let the band
be louder
than your voice
You are the lead singer
in your own life

Don't let the love song
to your soul
become a eulogy
for you are the creator
of words and melody

Don't let the soothing sound
of your steady breath
be smothered
and silenced
in your ego's cries for attention

You are the creator of your very own song
You decide whether it is short or long
You decide the rhythm, words and melody

You decide!
Sing your song!
Be brave!
Sing loud!
Be free!

Love-Eyes Exercise

Are you living the life you truly want or are you living someone else's dreams?

Love-Eyes Exercise

How easy is it for you to speak up
and say what you want to say?

Love-Eyes Exercise

How can you support yourself
when daring to speak up?

Love-Eyes Exercise

What helps you soothe your nervous system after you dare to sing loudly?

Love-Eyes Exercise

How do a fear of judgement and a fear of speaking up correlate?

HEARTBEAT

Listen to your heartbeat
echoing in the sacred halls
of your inner being
beating to the rhythm
of Love
empowering your soul

Breathe into
every pause

--

Let
the beat of the drum
ignite a trance

--

Feel the power
Feel the freedom
Feel the chance
to live your life
in unison
with the rhythm
of your soul's melody

Love-Eyes Exercise

How tuned are you to your intuition?

Love-Eyes Exercise

Where in your body do you feel
when something is right for you?

Love-Eyes Exercise

How can you strengthen your intuition?

Love-Eyes Exercise

When in your life have you made a decision based on intuition? Did the decision bring fruitful results? If not, can it be that it was based on other people's opinions?

ZOOM IN

Zoom in
and see
the whole world
in the close-up
of your soul
Stand still
and focus
on who you are
Look outside
by turning inside
inside out
outside in
flip
the image
drop
the struggle
and live your life
through
the magnificent
magnifier
of Love

Love-Eyes Exercise

How can you shift your focus towards Love?

Love-Eyes Exercise

Where can you witness beauty today?

Love-Eyes Exercise

Can you observe the effect of
"Where the focus goes, the energy flows."?

Love-Eyes Exercise

What can you observe closer?

Love-Eyes Exercise

Where is it needed to see the bigger picture, and zoom out?

PART IV:

I Am Love

Giving is easy.

Especially for us sensitive people, who like to take care of others, who are helpers, caregivers, teachers and leaders, giving comes naturally. Whether it is money, time or love; we mostly give it away generously.

What we don't notice is that it feels so easy because we have control. When we give, we can control how much we give, how long, to whom and when we stop. When we receive it gets harder. However, in a universe that is built on balance, giving and receiving needs to even out. Paired with our people-pleasing upbringing, we give until we burn out and nothing is left of us.

Our erroneous perception of what "love" is, often leads us to the desperate cry: When is it my turn? We feel like "love" is something that we get, something that we can give away, when Love actually is our source.

Love doesn't live inside us; we live inside Love.

When we ground ourselves and learn to silence our monkey mind, we can learn to bathe in the spirit of Love. Here we suddenly see the truth with clarity:

I AM LOVE!

WHAT IF

What if
there is no limit
of who you can be?

What if
the things you see
are not reality?

What if
truth
is a perception
alienated
by the patterns
that are woven so beautifully
into your being?

What if
faith
is the natural
source
that is circulating
in your blood
and you just
don't remember
to drink from it?

What if

Love
is safe
and you
just spend your whole life
trying to prove
that it is not?

What
if you changed
the plot?

What if
you make Love
the main character
in your life
and use
all the other ones
as mere means
to create
your
happily
ever
after?

What if?

Love-Eyes Exercise

What is your relationship with Love?

Love-Eyes Exercise

Where have you witnessed acts of Love?

Love-Eyes Exercise

Which relationship do you want to have with Love?

Love-Eyes Exercise

How would you love,
if you weren't afraid of getting hurt?

WHEN LOVE IS SERVED

Don't ask
why I love you

Ask yourself
why you
feel the need
to ask this question

Don't try to grasp
with your mind
what can only
be found
in the heart

When love is served
you don't ask for the price
you don't ask for the ingredients
you don't ask why the chef
felt inspired to serve it

Just indulge into it
let it nourish you
enjoy every bite
and don't be afraid
to find an empty plate
in the end

You usually don't refuse to eat
even if you know
that the plate will be empty
in the end, do you?

No, you know
that there's enough
for everyone
at any time,
no need to haste

Why deny yourself
savouring the taste?

Let me assure you,
Love is served
every single day
in many different ways

Love-Eyes Exercise

How easy is it for you to receive Love?

Love-Eyes Exercise

How do you make it difficult for others to love you?

Love-Eyes Exercise

What would your life look like
if you could easily receive Love?

Love-Eyes Exercise

If you receive Love,
does it feel enough to you?

Love-Eyes Exercise

How can you receive Love from yourself?

THE ALGORHYTHM OF LOVE

Love
is not a series
of little steps

She is an opening
through a thousand doors

Through mystery
and glowing souls
filling rivers, cups and bowls
up to the brim
towards the
overflow
of peace and bliss

She is
endless growth
she's not the how
she is the why
her kiss
is gentle, never shy
she doesn't impose
or lecture minds
she opens hearts
helps us unwind
the web of logic
to pathos she guides
she asks us to open
our hearts, oh so wide

for we are the love
that we carry inside

She begs us just to
flow along with her tide
she doesn't teach steps
she's spiralling up
swirling us round
never needing to stop

She's light and she's ease
She's joy and she's home
She's always there
never leaving us
alone

So, let's dance
to the sounds of the song
that Love is singing
to make us strong
Let us shake
Let us break
Let us cry
Let us fly
let us follow her
to the land
we've always
dreamed of
let us get caught
in the algorhythm
of Love

Love-Eyes Exercise

How can you let Love teach you how to love?

Love-Eyes Exercise

Where can you ask yourself:
What would Love do?

Love-Eyes Exercise

What would your life look like,
if Love showed up
in every thread of your life?

Love-Eyes Exercise

How can you feed the contagious energy of Love today?

Love-Eyes Exercise

How can you give Love?
How can you be Love?

INFINITY

Love
is the infinite
source
that runs through your veins
and comes forth
when you let it flow
when you give room
for the seed
to grow

Love is the never-ending
story
the happily ever after
that surrounds you
with its glory

You are born
as Love
and born
to love
and birthing Love
with every step
of the way

When you give Love
away
freely and without conditions
you can see
the frequent repetition
of the waves
she is creating

The Love
that is emanating
off your soul's
infinite well
lives inside you
inside your heart
your soul
and every tiny cell.

Love-Eyes Exercise

How can you make more room for Love?

Love-Eyes Exercise

What can you let go of today that is blocking you from receiving Love?

Love-Eyes Exercise

How can you be more unconditional?

Love-Eyes Exercise

How can you differ when you are pleasing people from when you are being unconditional?

Love-Eyes Exercise

What would your life look like
if you were in Love all the time?

Love-Eyes Exercise

What can you do to get there?

YOU ARE HERE TO FLY

Lift up your head
look around
you are here to fly

Straighten your back
roll your shoulders
let your body cry

Open your eyes
savour the beauty
lift your gaze upon the sky
Lay one hand on your heart
breathe in deeply

Can you feel your why?

Why are you here?
What makes you strive?
Who do you want to be?
What makes you come alive?

Clear your throat softly
strengthen your voice
There's no need to be shy

Shine all of your light
onto the world
until the day you die

Don't be afraid
Love comes with wings
for you are here to fly

Love-Eyes Exercise

How can you strengthen your faith to believe in something bigger than yourself?

Love-Eyes Exercise

Why do you think that
you are here on this earth?

Love-Eyes Exercise

When do you feel most alive?

Love-Eyes Exercise

How do you want to show up in this world?
How do you want to be remembered
when you leave this physical plane?

EPILOGUE

Once upon a time, the world was at peace. The wish to be happy was stronger than the hunger of the need to be right. Everyone knew that nobody was broken and that all was well in the world. Everybody recognized the creator in themselves and was courageously stepping onto their unique soul's journey. They were brave enough to embark on the biggest quest of cosmic intention - to show up as Love every day.

When they got upset, they were kind to themselves and to each other and communicated respectfully and non-violently. Wars, violence and hatred ceased to exist as people learned to be unconditional in their experience, trusting in the caring forces of the universe that would guide them through their lives. Love overflowed as abundance into the sacred convergence of everything. Every being on earth felt worthy and loveable and knew that they were already whole. Oneness was omnipresent, and every culture contributed their wisdom into the melting cauldron of unity. Respect was woven into a tapestry of diversity.

The innate beauty of all creation was celebrated in the wonder of awe. Gratitude was the unquenchable well of being, embraced by the awareness of humility. The air was quivering in laughter and music, wildly dancing to the poetic rhythm of creation.

Cheerful children's voices reverberated with the canyons as they beautifully explored their individuality in the school of life and studied the curriculum of human mystery. Teachers became students and students became teachers, willingly co-creating a web of understanding and compassion. Every human was free, and their very own songs created a mosaic symphony of harmony conducted by the power of Love.

AFTERWORD

We are all here to shine our light. When we step into our purpose and step onto the path of Love, we raise our vibration every day. Our aura shines brighter and we literally glow. It seems as if the light of our inner core penetrates our body and breaks through every cell, to expand into the light of our soul. We radiate Love in the most powerful way. The higher we rise, the smaller our shadow gets. However, the shadow will always be there and is needed, because without shadow there would be no light.

Yet, loving our shadow parts sometimes takes a lot of practice and patience. When our soul calls us to a greater mission, we often resist. Just like the heroes on their journey, who refuse the call in the beginning, knowing that the task ahead comes with loss. Loss of old stories, loss of old connections, of relationships, places, ideas, feelings and the loss of outdated versions of ourselves. In order to step into the unknown, we need to let go of the familiar life.

The ego is afraid of the unknown for it is here to keep us safe. The ego often steps in, trying to protect us. When our shadow steps in front of us, we become blind. We might feel blocked and cut off from our source. All we can do is to thank our ego and embrace it. If we push against it, it only gets bigger. If we meet our ego with self-compassion and kindness, it will melt into the light of Love.

As we trust in the bigger picture and the guidance of a higher power, we are able to step onto our path with grace, letting fear loosely flap in the wind. We can use a sail to choose our direction. Arms wide open, surrendering to the wind of change, we embark towards new horizons. Love is our compass. Faith is our foundation in the big wide ocean of adventures. Knowing that when a storm comes, our wings will lift us up into the skies, where we will surf the clouds towards eternity. Melting into the heavens of One.

ACKNOWLEDGEMENTS

As I wrote in the beginning of the book, if I had to give credit to everyone who inspired me to write these lines, I would have to list everyone I have interacted with in this life and in other lifetimes. Thus, I will just list the ones that are directly involved with the writing process of this book. I want to thank my friends, family and former colleagues for always believing in me and my creativity. Your encouragement means the world to me and always keeps me going, no matter what. A special thanks to my parents, who nourished my love for words in my earliest years through trips to the library and reading.

I am deeply grateful for the wonderful teachers I had at school and for a dear school friend, who encouraged me to write and share my words. After so many years, the words finally found me again through the help of spirit, who led me home into the arms of Love.

A big thank you to my Instagram tribe and to my Substack, Medium and E-Mail list readers for their ongoing support of my words and the Love that they are spreading. I thank the Creative Mindfulness Community for the always kind support and inspiration. A special thank you to Emily O'Neal, the writer of this book's foreword. I deeply appreciate your ongoing spiritual and creative support and our shared Love for fairies and poetry.

I also have to thank the universe and my guides for sending me the very situation that fueled my passion to write this book. I thank Love for teaching me how to love myself so much that I was able to learn to create instead of react.

Thank you to Ainslie MacLeod and his Spirit Guides who encouraged me to write every day. It was this very door that let me find back into the world of words.

Much gratitude to Tanya Markul, who introduced me to all the joys of self-publishing in her amazing online course. Some poems in this book were created within this exploration of book publishing and my inner world.

I thank Derek Murphy for the formatting template of this book, it made the self-publishing process a lot easier. Thank you, Bethany Atazadeh for your insightful YouTube

Videos on how to self-publish. I appreciate the generous gesture of making the content available for free!

I also want to thank other brave self-publishers. Your courage to put your words out there let my wish to follow your example grow stronger every day. All of our voices are needed out there!

Finally, I thank you, dear reader, for holding this book in your hand and hopefully sharing the wor(l)ds.

Most importantly, I need to thank poetry. It was poetry who lovingly reflected my true authentic self in the mirror of words. Poetry has been my companion, my best friend, my lover and my guide. Poetry touched me in the creases of my soul and smoothed out the sharp edges of old patterns and beliefs. Poetry is the adventure of my life(times), my happy place and always helps me to show up as the best version of myself. Poetry never ceases to fail to guide me home to the Love that I am. Alongside poetry I don't just walk through life. I fly.

Thank you so much for reading this book! It would mean the world to me if you could leave a short review and let me know what you enjoyed about the poetry, the questions and the words in this book!

ABOUT THE AUTHOR

"I am Love, therefore I write."

Nicole Rank is the creator of Love-Eyes Spiritual Development and the human who brought this book into being. She is also a holistic and accredited Creative Mindfulness teacher, and an intuitive guide who provides Co-Creative Coaching, retreats and courses.

Nicole is also a poet, writer, tree-hugger and Love herald. After teaching at a public school in Germany for 13 years, Nicole took a leap of faith. In 2023, she gathered her books, candles, favourite mugs and her surprised cats. She crammed all of it into her little car and drove off towards the luscious greens of Ireland. Here she has resided ever since, living the questions that Love asks her, every single day.

Sadhbh Adamea is Nicole's pen name. The name Sadhbh is Irish and found her as her very own soul was reunited with her and ignited the flame of her true essence. Visiting Ireland for the first time (in this life) she instantly felt like home and also had a very magical encounter with a fawn in the luscious green forests of Ross Castle.

The deer accompanied Nicole as a spirit guide since then and she deeply resonated with the meaning of the name Sadhbh. The name is not only considered the goddess of the deer, but also stands for transformation, change, shapeshifting, motherhood and Love.

The Irish myth about Sadhbh, the woman who was transformed into a deer, talks about a painful but beautiful journey to Love. The deer here finds her strength to adapt and survive in her new form.

Like Sadhbh, Nicole is not taking nature for granted and loves to witness moments of awe that nature provides in abundance. Once she stepped into her own authenticity, Nicole was reunited with her essence: Love. Since then, she has devoted her life to sharing everything she knows about Love.

The name Adamea mainly stands for magnetic love energy. In Spanish, "adamar" means "I love greatly." As Nicole's soul clearly is on a mission of Love this name stands for the mantra which she practices every day: I am Love.

Having a pen name is part of a ritual that gets Nicole into a receiving mode which allows her to write from the depths of her soul. It is a magic cloak that she slips on while her heart creates poetry, prose and essays from the letter labyrinth of the keyboard.

Find more of Sadhbh's poetry on:

Substack: @sadhbhadamea

Instagram: @sadhbh.adamea

LOVE-EYES SPIRITUAL DEVELOPMENT

Love-Eyes Spiritual Development is located in Ireland and is a company that provides heartful spiritually focused retreats, online and in-person training as well as coaching that nurtures you to come home to Love. You can find more information as well as online courses on the website **www.love-eyes.com.**

If you want to get inspiration or stay updated on events, mindfulness and meditation, you can follow Nicole here, too:

Instagram: @onlylovecanhealtheworld

Substack: @loveeyes

YouTube: @Love-EyesSD

SUGGESTED READINGS

Here is a list of my favourite poets:

- Jamie Millard
- Rumi
- Rainer Maria Rilke
- Oriah Mountain Dreamer
- Richard Wagamese
- Nikita Gill
- Morgan Harper Nichols
- David Whyte
- Romy Wyser
- Tanya Markul

DEAR SOUL FRIEND

If you are interested in collaboration, please feel free to reach out. Together we can move mountains and make the world a better place! I thank you very much for reading these lines! Please share your experiences with this book, I would love to witness the creativity it sparked in you. If you need more inspiration on poetry, meditation or mindfulness practices, head over to my website to the resources section.

Reach out to me via: **loveyes.sd@gmail.com**

Want To Read More?

Download my free E-Book:

"How To Love Life ...

... and let life love you (even more)"

This E-Book includes guidance, poetry, resources, exercises, journal pages, audio files and tips for you to come home to Love!

Download it here:

Manufactured by Amazon.ca
Acheson, AB

16477794R00101